THE VETERAN'S WORK BOOK

How to Transition Out of the Military and GET HIRED!

KEVIN LACZ
BILL HOBBS &
LINDSEY LACZ

The La Plata Press
La Plata, MD

This book, or parts thereof, offers suggestions
believed to be helpful and useful based upon the author's experience
and research. Nothing in this book should be considered to be an ab-
solute statement about a specific course of action to be taken in any
particular circumstance, as numerous factors must be considered. This
book is not intended to offer any legal advice or counsel, and to the
extent that any legal issues are referenced in this book,
it is not intended to be a substitute for professional legal
representation.

ISBN: 978-0-9858456-7-4
e-book: 978-0-9858456-8-1

For More Information About

The WORK Book

Books, Learning Materials, and Lecture Series

www.theworkbookseries.com

Executive Editor Charles Hobbs

WHEN I FIRST READ *The WORK Book* two-years ago, I immediately realized there was a need for a similar book for veterans transitioning out of the military. As a speaker, I regularly meet veterans who ask, "How were you able to make the transition from Navy SEAL to Physician Assistant?" They are impressed, not just that I went back to school and found a new career, but that I'm well-adjusted to life in the civilian world. The more veterans I meet, the more I realize the need for a discussion about how to make that seamless transition from active duty service member to life after the military.

Bill Hobbs's first version of *The WORK Book* was wildly successful and provides a valuable asset to students entering the job force for the first time. For the Veteran Edition, we teamed up with the aim of repurposing some of his material specifically for service members transitioning out of the military and into a new career. Although everyone undergoes the DoD's mandatory TAP course before separation, we feel there is more we can provide to veterans venturing out on their post-military journey.

It is my opinion that veterans with military experience are valuable assets in the business world because they have experience leading, being led, and performing under pressure. However, it's necessary for veterans to learn how to function in their new environment. Just as I meet many veterans who ask how they can use their military experience to their advantage, I regularly meet civilians who ask how they can better relate to veterans. Increasingly, I meet employers who ask what they can do to accommodate veterans in the workplace because often there is a disconnect between veterans and civilians. It's well-documented that veterans often feel they don't relate well to civilians and that civilians often don't understand veterans. I ask veterans to assume some responsibility for rectifying this situation. As a group, they should remember that military service neither automatically guarantees or disqualifies a candidate for a particular position. A veteran should be a highly adaptable human being and should be able to function in the same work environment as his/her peers without requiring special accommodations. A person's time in the service should make him/her *more* employable, not hinder an employer's ability to hire that person. In order for that to be true, veterans must learn how to brand their experiences and assimilate into civilian life. My views may vary wildly from many others, but I attribute much of my post-military success to my willingness to *become* a civilian. You may find a bit of tough love sprinkled throughout the pages of this WORK Book, but I encourage you to respect your time in the military for what it was, to look back on it fondly, provided it was a positive experience for you, and begin your journey into the civilian world with a clean slate and an open mind.

CONTENTS

INTRODUCTION

I EMBARKED ON A twisted path toward a career as a medical provider in the fall of 2000. As a freshman at James Madison University, I enrolled in the necessary pre-med courses and imagined I was preparing myself to become a doctor. By then end of my freshmen year, I found I had spent more time in the Rugby House basement than in the classroom and that I had not made great academic progress toward graduation.

With the fall of 2001, came a watershed moment in my 20-year-old life. My close friend's father was killed in the South Tower of the World Trade Center on September 11, 2001. At that point, I had a desire to do something bigger and more important with my life. I was able-bodied and angry about the terrorist attacks, so I joined the Navy. I wanted to see combat.

After 8 years in the military, during which I did two combat deployments to Iraq as a Navy SEAL, I felt like I fulfilled my obligation to my country. I still had a deep-seated desire to practice medicine, and as an 18D medic, I'd been able to at least begin down that path in the military. I believed it was time for me to rejoin the civilian world and embark on a second career.

I was fortunate to be able to make the transition from the military to UCONN, to graduate school, and finally, to the workforce. That's not to say it was easy, but I knew I had the skills to make it happen. I meet and speak to veterans all the time who ask how they can do the same thing. How can they leave the service and go to college as nontraditional students? How can they find jobs in the private sector? With this work book, I take a holistic approach to realistically prepare veterans for the difficulties of the hiring process by empowering them to utilize all of their available resources. While the Transition Assistance Program has certainly become more robust since I left Active Duty in 2008, this workbook takes an extra step towards addressing veterans' current and future transitional needs in terms of personal branding, acclimating to civilian life, and entering the job market. Since professional growth and building a personal brand are continuous processes, this book also helps veterans grow after they find a new career. *The Veterans' WORK Book* addresses all of these needs and is short enough that veterans can read it quickly and apply it immediately.

CHAPTER ONE

PERSONAL BRANDING

MANY RESOURCES EXIST TO aid in the transition from active duty service member to member of the civilian community. As you prepare to complete your time of service, you will attend Transition Assistance Program (TAP) courses. Your TAP manual, the staff at the Military Services transition office, and the staff you are assigned to at the VA center are valuable resources you should be prepared to take advantage of. If you are a recently separated veteran, the same resources will be useful to you as you adjust to your new life. Attending TAPs may feel like just another mandatory training the military sends you through or the last stop before you are released from Active Duty, but consider it the bare minimum amount of preparation you should do before going out into the civilian workforce. If you want to get ahead, you should take advantage of every opportunity afforded to you, and that includes TAPs.

Although the DoD and the VA have provided you with some resources, in *The WORK Book* we take a holistic approach to your new life in the civilian labor force. One important aspect of this transition is your personal brand. Think of your personal brand as simply a reflection of the way you are viewed by others in the market. Right now, several of your peers in the military possess many of the same skills and qualifications as you. As you enter the private sector, however, you will find that those same skills and experiences make you distinct and separate you from others without military experience who are competing for the same job. Successful transition involves utilizing the valuable components of your past in order to sell your personal brand to prospective employers in the civilian world.

Take a few minutes to think about your military experience. What training and skills differentiate you from your competition in the marketplace, particularly those without military experience?

The following questions may also be useful when considering and expanding on the elements of your current personal brand:

► What job experiences have you had?

► What schools or training have you attended in the military?

► Are you a member of any clubs outside of work?

► Are you active in the community as a coach or volunteer?

► Have you been involved in sports or academic competitions?

► Have you ever held any leadership roles?

► Have you won any awards or recognition?

► Have you attended any school outside of the military?

Compile any paperwork that documents any of the above (DD-214, Training Record, Service Record, DD Form 2586, any diplomas or transcripts, etc.). Think about how these experiences help shape who you are today. Later we will talk about how to package these unique qualities to increase your brand value to a potential employer.

The process of building an effective personal brand works much like the process of building an effective product brand. In the case of a product brand, the market has a perception of the value of that brand, what it's "known for," and consumers make buying decisions based on that perceived value. Some of the best brand marketing companies in the world are currently employed by energy drinks. Many energy drinks build brands around their products that make us think of excitement, extreme sports, amazing music, and real people pushing the limits of time and space. These marketers create incredible content around their companies' brands. They constantly manage the message of the brand and shape that message to connect with the intended audience.

Like these top products, developing your personal brand is a similar process. It may not require the same level of investment, but it does require you to consider the same elements of your brand. That is, just as these energy drinks' marketers create content around their brand and constantly manage and shape their message, you can fuel your personal brand by continually creating relevant content and frequently monitoring and shaping the message of your brand. In the SEAL Teams we used to say, "Plan your dive and dive your plan." A successful transition out of the military and into the workforce is the same. You need to begin the process of building a personal brand for your civilian life now to ensure success in your post-military life.

The following pages contain exercises and information that can be used to help shape your personal brand as you embark on your new life post military. Use the resources available to you, in addition to your TAP Manual, transition counselor, or VA case manager to mold your brand into something attractive enough to sell to your future employer. As a member of the military, you have become accustomed to a certain level of conformity and anonymity. However, as you rejoin the civilian world, you will need to sell your individuality.

You may have spent your entire military career trying to be a gray man, but when it comes to your résumé on a hiring manager's desk, you need to stand out. Hiring managers are often pressed for time when reviewing résumés, so you need to stand out as uniquely valuable. Statistically, only 26% of US employers see veterans as a strategic asset to the team,[1] so it's important you sell yourself as a qualified candidate

---

[1] Zoroya, Gregg: Employer survey: Veterans viewed as heroes, but not necessarily a good hire, July 7, 2016, USA Today; News.

who also has military experience rather than an out of work veteran. Your military service will often earn you a handshake and a "thank you for your service," but you will still need to compete with everyone else when it comes to the actual hiring process. You may not have ever written a real résumé before. That's ok. They are important to the hiring process, but we don't want your résumé to be the only data point that an employer uses to decide whether to hire you. You can find examples of résumé formats in the appendix of this book; however, stylistic elements are constantly changing and résumés, candidate videos, and e-résumés simply represent a medium for delivery rather than the branding elements that are critical from a content standpoint. Ultimately, a résumé should include your contact information, content on your experience, training, awards, and links to portfolios and other media. Your résumé should not be a regurgitation of your entire DD 214 or Training Record. Most recruiters spend 6 seconds or less the first time they view a résumé. Therefore, the general rule is that a résumé should be as short as possible while conveying a candidate's relevant experience. It's still generally accepted that most résumés should be one page in length, possibly two if the candidate has extensive experience.

Don't be afraid to ask for help with your résumé. You can visit www.vets.gov to build a basic résumé if you cannot find help in person from a case manager, friend, or counselor. We, however, will focus on ensuring that the content and experience is representative of your true brand value. The best thing to do may be to show your résumé to a civilian friend and ask for honest advice. Don't underestimate the importance of having a well-formatted, relevant résumé. It may be the difference between you being called for an interview or not.

Do not assume that being called for an interview means that the hiring managers you will meet have done a lot of research on you. They may only glance at your résumé and do a quick digital search right before meeting with you. The stronger your brand presence, the better chance you have of making a positive impression before you even step into the interview.

A lot of books focus their content on the interview, framing it as the "most important part of the process." Interviews are critically important, but they are only a small part of the hiring process. You can build your brand in a way that says great things about you long before you ever sit down for an interview, and your unique personal brand can help to accelerate your progress long after you are hired.

Chances are, while you were in the military you were conscious of your online presence because of certain rules and guidelines about what you could or could not post to your social media accounts. When you get out of the military, you may be tempted to use your new freedom to post all of the things you couldn't post while you were in. Remember that your digital footprint is difficult to erase, so it is very important to understand, shape, and manage your digitally available information and messaging. I have heard a lot of stories about people who have lost opportunities because of the information that a simple search revealed. Be aware that anything you post, write, or comment could be seen by the entire world. The same can be true of the application process for college. Be aware of everything you post, Tweet, share, etc. Your posts could be used as an argument for not hiring or admitting you.

On the other hand, when shaped correctly, a digital presence can actually be a very positive contribution to your brand depending on the career you seek. Social media can be an incredibly helpful tool for showcasing your talents and networking with others in your field of interest. As you create a portfolio of your work, you can grow a following that may potentially lead to other opportunities. It's important to have patience and remain professional when you are using social media as a tool for personal branding.

Creating your own website is another way to improve your brand. A professional website can become a central point of reference for your personal brand. It allows you to more easily control messaging about who you are professionally, display your work and projects, display your successes and partnerships, and create a single thread to tie together your related professional interests.

From your website, you can link to other sites where you have built elements of your overall brand presence. For example, if you are working toward a career in automotive restoration and you love classic muscle cars, you might begin a blog that links back to a website you have created on car shows you attend. Both sites would showcase your knowledge of cars and build on additional elements of your brand. You may even become a contributor for a digital publisher that already has a great presence and, if permitted, link back to your website.

You can also utilize other elements of your brand that don't directly relate to your field of interest but illustrate your commitment to learning and growing professionally to display your depth to prospective employers. For example, your skills as a painter, a tutor, or a jewelry designer may not obviously connect to a career in management consulting; however, showing progress in these areas still contribute to your brand. They help to paint a picture of your interests and accomplishments while revealing a fascinating and fun side of your personal brand, thus separating you from other candidates.

The VA Can Be a Great Resource

As you read *The Veterans' WORK Book* and transition to civilian life, remember one of your best resources is your VA Case Manager. Make an appointment to meet this person as early as possible and stay in touch regularly. He or she will guide you through the maze of programs offered by the VA, many of which are not obviously available when you first leave the military. If you decide to seek higher education, these people will help enroll you in the GI Bill or Vocational Rehabilitation. If you make an effort to get to know them personally, most of them will guide you as you choose classes, build skill sets, and set forth toward careers that will set you apart long after you separate from the military. These professionals have great experience and can help you shape your raw ideas into a finely tuned personal brand.

Of course, many VA Centers are overcrowded, and your case manager will probably be busy and overworked. Remember, ultimately you are responsible for your future, so you should come to these meetings prepared with questions and ideas so that your case manager can help you efficiently. It's not your case manager's job to fix everything for you. Being prepared will allow you to get the most out of your discussions. The relationships, experience, and interactive collaboration can prove invaluable as you build your personal brand.

Although the VA hasn't been without its issues in the past, I will say that it served me well in my transitional years from the Navy. I developed a relationship with my case manager at the center in North Haven, CT. She stuck with me, enrolling me in the GI Bill so I could attend UCONN, later helping me apply for Vocational Rehab, and eventually transferring my case to North Carolina when I got into Wake Forest. She even checked in on me periodically after that. These people want to help you, but you have to help them do it. Show up at medical, keep in touch with your case manager, and do some research on the programs that are available to you.

As you begin this exciting process toward a new life, remember this is a new beginning!

Tips:

► Get help writing your first résumé after your separate from the military.

► Be very careful regarding what you post or share online.

► Utilize the programs the VA has to offer. My greatest blessing after I got out was the Vocational Rehabilitation & Employment (VR&E) program. If you are rated at least 20% disabled, you can apply for benefits to cover the cost of vocational training. For me, that meant Physician Assistant School.

► Stay current with all of your VA appointments, especially medical. My partial discectomy and laminectomy in 2012 were related to an injury I sustained in BUD/S in 2003, but since everything was well-documented, my process with the VA since then has been relatively smooth.

CHAPTER TWO
THE JOURNEY

Leaving the military can conjure a mixture of emotions. For many service members, the military is the major (if not sole) professional experience of their adult lives. It's more than a job — it's a lifestyle in which we build relationships, experience life changing events, and enjoy the certain amount of security that comes with the terms of an enlistment. You have likely grown and matured a great deal during your time as a service member. While the prospect of the freedom to live where you want, make more money, and perhaps be home with your family regularly may be exciting, it's not unusual to be overwhelmed by the fact that you are leaving behind the life you've been committed to for the past several years.

Take the time to mourn your military career. Whether you served six years or twenty-six, your life is about to change. To become truly happy and subsequently successful in your new life, you need to fully accept that your time as an active duty member of the United States Military has come to an end and that what you do from here on will never be the same as what you did when you were in. Take some time to reflect on what your time in the service has meant to you. It will always be a part of who you are, and as you transition out, you will join a club even larger than the active duty military: veterans.

Most veterans are very proud of their service, and that's great! You can be proud of your past while looking forward to the future. Part of a successful transition is embracing your new role, and you will transition most successfully if you realize that things are done differently in the civilian world. It is your new job to learn those ways. I travel all over the country and meet veterans everywhere I go. The most successful veterans I meet are the ones who got out of the military and jumped right into learning to survive in the civilian world. The ones who seem to struggle the most are the veterans who cling to their service and wrestle with accepting that they are no longer in the military. They feel lost, and although these veterans often do not want to hear it, I tell them they need to move forward into their new lives and accept the responsibility of assimilating to the civilian world. Veterans make up about 7% of the US population, with post 9-11 veterans making up a tiny percentage of that number. It's more reasonable for us to conform to the other 93% of the population than to expect 93% to accommodate 7%.

There is, however, a difference between moving on and moving forward. I look back at my years as a SEAL as some of the best of the years of my life with the greatest men I have ever known. I keep in touch with people I served with regularly, I think about my time in the Navy often, and I know that my military service greatly influenced me as I became an adult. When I got out, however, I was eager to meet the next challenge head on and find success. I knew that would be impossible if I refused to see myself as a civilian.

Anxiety and apprehension are normal parts of new experiences. The more open your mind is as you approach this transition, the easier this transition will be. Develop a clear understanding of what you want to accomplish, starting with identifying the right career path, and any anxiety will melt away.

Choosing a career path that interests you and allows you to learn, develop, and grow as a professional, can make a big difference in your overall happiness and ability to succeed.

Tips:

► As your military career ends, take the time to mourn it.

► Examine what being a civilian means to you and prepare yourself to conform to the other 93% of the population.

CHAPTER THREE
Choices

WHEN YOU DECIDE TO separate from the military, there are more factors to consider than simply leaving Active Duty. You should start with the big picture elements and then work down to the smaller, more detailed elements. A new career is probably the source of the most stress, so you should start by choosing a field to pursue and then consider other factors such as where to live, your compensation, and your schedule.

You should certainly try to choose a career you will enjoy, but be sure to consider which skills you have developed in the military. Many of them are most likely transferable to a civilian profession. If you work in IT in the military, for example, it will probably be easier to stay in tech than attempt to cross into sales.

Below is a quick worksheet to help you channel your thoughts. Often, seeing things on paper helps to clarify ideas and solidify your choices. Think through each section, and write your answers.

If you are planning to enter a parallel field to your military job such as medicine, technology, or a skilled trade, then you have already chosen your field. However, you may want to narrow down the job type or even industry. If you are undecided on the type of field to enter, you should first spend some time reflecting on your interests, previous experience, education, and general skills. Certain jobs may require an education level that you have not yet attained, but you could work toward those requirements by using your VA Benefits.

Once you have chosen a field, you need to consider the career options available to you in that field. Read job descriptions within that field, and consider whether you could see yourself in that position. Use the Internet to find out what types of jobs are available and where they are concentrated.

Some jobs will be available everywhere, but other job types like manufacturing, IT, or Import/ Export jobs will have hubs where large concentrations of a particular job type exist. Many veterans find jobs in the government or contracting, and these positions are often concentrated around military installations.

As you work through your options, you should consider what additional resources you have that could be helpful during your search. A great place to start is your transition counselor or VA case manager. You should have access to one or both of these people, and they should be able to offer you some guidance in terms of viable career choices in relation to your skillset. These people see other service members in your position all the time and have helped many others just like you. Don't be shy about seeking the advice of these professionals. Walk them through your goals and share your worksheets so that you both understand the factors affecting your decision. You can also reach out to other veterans and ask for their advice and input.

Use the rest of the worksheet to work through other factors of consideration.

▶ What fields are most interesting to me?

A. _____

B. _____

C. _____

D. _____

E. _____

▶ What types of positions are available in these fields given my level of experience?

A. _____

B. _____

C. _____

D. _____

E. _____

► Which industries most appeal to me?

A. _____

B. _____

C. _____

D. _____

E. _____

► What types of positions (job titles) or job requirements fit my level of experience, education, and skill set?

A. _____

B. _____

C. _____

D. _____

E. _____

▶ Where are the majority of these opportunities located?

A. _____

B. _____

C. _____

D. _____

E. _____

▶ Am I able to live in the areas with high concentrations of opportunities?

☐ Yes   ☐ No   ☐ Maybe

▶ If not, can I work remotely?

☐ Yes   ☐ No   ☐ Maybe

▶ What are my long-term career goals?

A. _____

B. _____

C. _____

D. _____

E. _____

▶ Is this type of career a financially viable option for me right now?

    ☐ Yes   ☐ No   ☐ Maybe

▶ How can I better prepare myself to increase my chances of securing employment?

A. _____

B. _____

C. _____

D. _____

E. _____

As you write down the answers to these questions, consider how they affect your decision. If you are really serious about working in a particular field, you will need to make up your mind that you are going to give one-hundred percent to your new career. You will need to master new skills and continuously reevaluate your progress.

Tips:

▸ Consider jobs that translate easily from your rate or MOS in the military.

▸ Before pursuing a position, consider where the majority of those opportunities are located and whether they pay enough for you to realistically consider them.

CHAPTER FOUR
MONEY MATTERS

IT'S NO SECRET THAT military jobs, particularly for enlisted personnel, often don't pay as well as their civilian equivalents. Often when it comes time to transition out of the military, a service member has to ask, "How much should salary impact my decision to take a new job?" Honestly, the answer to the question is different for everyone. Every person walks a different path, and individual circumstances affect career decisions.

When I first got out of the military, I knew that my path was to Physician Assistant School. Before Physician Assistant School, I had to complete my undergraduate degree. While I was in undergraduate school, I worked at a driving school and taught off-road driving with nonstandard vehicles. I used skills I gained as a Navy SEAL to land a job I could work while I pursued my education.

At various points while I was an undergraduate and graduate student, I got calls from friends offering me contracting jobs in the security world. I turned all of them down with the exception of working as a technical adviser on

American Sniper. None of these positions placed my value even on par with where I had been as a SEAL, despite the hefty payday they promised. There was no guarantee for upwards mobility or a guarantee for further employment past the end of the contract. In my opinion, the work I was doing towards my Masters of Medical Science was more valuable to my personal brand than the short-term payoff of a security contract.

Find a job that you believe aligns with your value, and that may help answer your question about salary. Where do you want to be in 5 or 10 years, and what job will help you get there? It's easy to leave the military and feel pigeonholed into the contracting world. There's nothing wrong with contracting if you really *want* to do it, but you shouldn't feel like you *have* to do it. I enjoyed my time as a driving instructor, but I probably could have stayed there for years without much opportunity for upward mobility. You may experience something similar in the security contracting world – the money seems great when you first leave the military, but contracting does not necessarily guarantee a stable career, medical benefits, or security for your dependents.

Do not be afraid to pursue the training or education necessary to begin a career that will afford you some upward mobility. In the military, you were expected to make rank and promote. In the civilian world, there are plenty of opportunities for you to increase your pay and get promotions. Avoid the low hanging fruit of the easiest opportunity that comes your way as soon as you get out. If you invest in yourself and your new career, it will pay off in the long run. As a veteran, you have earned the benefits of the GI Bill and other educational opportunities. If your dream is to enter a career that requires a degree, now is your chance to work towards it. I cannot stress enough the value of being able to graduate debt free from undergraduate or graduate school. Pursuing an education will often increase your brand value and can buy you time if you're not sure what you want to do.

What you do from the time you leave the military forward should be a combination of fulfilling your dreams and fulfilling your obligations. I do believe that people should fulfill their dreams, but I also believe that people should handle their responsibilities. Maybe deep down you've always wanted to be a writer, but you have a wife and four kids. Now might not be the best time to quit working completely to start your first novel. Perhaps instead, you can use your education benefits toward a degree in journalism and compromise by working for a newspaper or magazine. Eventually, you may be able to write that novel.

Tips:

▶ Choose a job that you believe aligns with your value and that offers you some opportunity for upward mobility over the next several years.

▶ Strongly consider using your education benefits to work on a degree, particularly if there is a career you want to pursue that requires more than your current education level.

CHAPTER FIVE
FIT FIRST

As you transition out of the military, it's important to have the right mindset. A lot of service members view going on terminal leave and their separation date as the end goal, but you should really view this time of your life as a marathon, not a sprint. You are about to embark on a dramatic change of pace that may take you months, or even years, to fully adjust to. Take it slow, and realize that your new life may take some time to feel normal.

When I left active duty, I had almost two months of terminal leave before I started the spring semester at UCONN. I took that time to adjust to life outside of the military, to get used to being home with my fiancée every day, and to make plans for the future. By the time I began classes as an undergraduate, I realized that the best way for me to be successful in my civilian life and career was to move forward from my life in the military. That's not to say I couldn't talk about being a veteran or maintain the relationships I formed while I was in, but it was necessary to realize the difference between my former and current lives.

What is most important throughout the transition process is having realistic expectations. You want to really understand what you expect from your new life and job and what your prospective employer expects from you.

As you begin your job search, you must prepare for the interview process. Just as separating from the military is not all there is to transitioning, "winning the job" is not all there is to successful employment. Getting hired is the easy part. Keeping the job and building a successful career is much more difficult. The harder you work to build mutual understanding between your prospective employer and yourself, the more likely you'll find the right "fit." "Fit" is arguably the most important factor toward building a successful future post-military. *Fit* is a term that describes how well you align with a company's strategy, structure, and culture. It is important that you consider fit when seeking employment because if you take a job at the wrong company and end up bored, miserable, stressed out, or in complete disagreement with the company culture, you may end up wanting to quit and will be right back at the beginning of your job search.

Fit is important for employers, as well. They need to hire candidates who will be happy in their work environments and hopefully build careers with them. No employer wants to devote thousands of dollars in resources and training to have a new hire quit in six months. If you do not get hired after an interview, consider that it might not have been the right fit and trust that a better opportunity is waiting.

The search for the right fit begins long before the face-to-face interview. When you joined the military, you walked into the recruiter's office and held most of the cards, provided there was no reason to disqualify you for service. Now, you need to realize that employers hold most of the cards. They search for referral applicants, scan résumés, hire professional recruiters, and check references. Fit was a much smaller concern for the military, because the military planned to mold you to its standards for the duration of your contract. In the civilian world, employees are not bound by the same types of contracts; therefore, employers use many measures to increase their chances of making a successful, permanent hire. You must maximize your chances for success and happiness with a new company as well. Begin your research early, and don't let yourself "settle" because you will waste valuable time doing something that doesn't make you happy. As previously discussed, spend some time talking with a transition counselor or VA case manager to see if he or she can help you with any possible leads for companies and hiring managers that fit your search.

Also, be sure to look at your contacts and social media to see if you have any relationships that can help you find potential employers. Talk to friends who have already gotten out of the military, especially if they were a similar MOS/AFSC/Rate as you.

Career fairs are another way to meet a lot of potential employers and learn about their companies in a short period of time. The face-to-face aspect of the career fair gives you an opportunity to talk with potential hiring managers and build your network. If you make a great impression with them at a job fair, it's reasonable to believe that you will have a better chance of securing a follow-up interview. Some job fairs are specifically geared toward military/veteran candidates. You can easily find these events on websites such as recruitmilitary.com. Immediately email any companies you like, thank them for the time, and ask about a follow-up interview.

Reflect on the time you have spent thinking about fit. Research and develop a list of all the companies that fit the description of what you are looking for. Then locate job openings that are available within each company and note the link to the listing on the worksheet below.

List of Potential Companies with Job openings

Company	Website or Job Link

1. Company Name _____

Link _____

2. Company Name _____

Link _____

3. Company Name _____

Link _____

4. Company Name _____

Link _____

5. Company Name _____

Link _____

6. Company Name _____

Link _____

Now, prioritize the openings in order from your top to least favorite options.

Order of Companies from First Choice to Last Choice Worksheet

Rank   Company Name

1. _____

2. _____

3. _____

4. _____

5. _____

6. _____

Now you have a target list and know exactly what is available. Set that list aside for a moment, and be sure that you are actually ready to begin applying. You need to understand that everything you do regarding your career is a representation of you. You are your own brand, and your brand either gains value or loses value based on your choices. New employers know very little about you and will view you based on the limited information they have. If you have a great résumé, great references, and you develop a good rapport before the interview, employers will be more likely to view your brand as valuable and hire you. This is because they can only base their initial opinion of you on these things. Conversely, if you have a poorly written résumé, no references, and have never spoken to any of the interviewers, employers will base their initial opinion of you on your poorly written résumé. They will not even waste the time to check your references or give you an interview.

CHAPTER SIX

REPRESENTATIVE RÉSUMÉS

A RÉSUMÉ IS THE first representation of you and your brand that any employer will see. It is critical that the résumé looks professional and includes all the necessary contacts and your work history, but your résumé should be much more than that. An employer could potentially search through thousands of résumés for a single position, so you have to find a way to make yours stand out and impress the person reading it. When attempting to enter the civilian workforce, the first step is to master the appropriate language. Many employers use word searches to narrow the pool into a smaller group with reasonably similar skill sets. If you want to be included in the smaller group, your résumé needs to include the right words. For example, if you want to be hired as a landscape architect, there might be some key words like "Landscape", "Architect", "Designer", "Natural", "Outdoor", "Trees", etc. that employers search for electronically in the stack of résumés. They may then look for specific certifications, education background, or experience requirements to further narrow the pool. Typically, once the pool is narrowed, a real person will finally read the remaining résumés to look for possible candidates to interview over the phone or in person. Once your résumé is in someone's hands, it will need to attract that person's attention. This means that your résumé should not only look professional and be formatted properly but that it should address the skills that employers are searching for. When writing your résumé, scrub it of any acronyms or phrases that you know are exclusive to military. Do some research to find out if any of your certifications or qualifications have civilian equivalents that you can note. It is also a good idea to have a friend look your résumé over before you send it out.

It is likely you have some training and skills that may not be relevant to the job you are applying for. Remember that most employers still expect your résumé to be about a page long and they will only spend a few seconds reading it. If you are applying for work as a delivery truck driver, for example, you probably do not need to waste space on your résumé listing your rifle qualifications. You would be better served using that space to describe your Driver Mechanic Badge, any special driving schools you attended, or something else of relevance.

My wife did some résumé work for a couple of Army dog handlers who were applying for work on a defense contract. Their résumés were each 4-6 pages long, listed every single training they had ever attended in their 12+ years in the Army, and were a mess of acronyms and military jargon. Assume the people reading your résumé have never been in the military and only have time to read the most relevant information. What do you want to show them in those few moments?

It is perfectly acceptable to have different versions of your résumé for different job applications if the jobs focus on different skill sets. Look back at your DD 214 or service record and pull out any relevant training or experiences.

One way to find some of the skills that are important for a specific job type is to look at job postings online. In the requirements section of a job posting, companies will detail the skills required for that type of position. As you look at ten to fifteen examples, themes will start to emerge. For example, if you want to become a manager for a tech company, some of the postings will include things like "experience managing people", "familiarity with CRM software", "three years minimum in the field of...", "excellent communication skills", and "ability to provide meaningful feedback". From these listings, you can glean words or skills that are applicable to include in your résumé. The key is to arrange the words in a way that highlight the skills you have with the work you have done. For example,

▶ If you were the LPO of your last platoon, but didn't hold the position for three years, you could still highlight your experience as a supervisor and include the responsibility you held over a period of time. In particular, be sure to highlight the number of people and how much equipment you managed. You might say, "Oversaw 16 platoon members for a period of 15 months, wrote and submitted evaluations for review by Officer in Charge, managed four departments with equipment worth x million dollars, etc."

► If you were a cannon crewmember (13B) in the Army and the requirement is good communication skills, you might say, "Built strong relationships with other crewmembers and communicated verbally, non-verbally, and via wire and radio to effectively support ground combat operations."

In either example, you may not have the exact skills outlined in the requirements section, but you can highlight the skills and experience that you do have that make you a strong candidate.

Another important element to a strong résumé is the story that your various jobs tell. If you were promoted to E5 in the Army in fewer than 4 years, or chosen as LPO over more senior NCOs, you should note that. Many people's résumés lack a story. Some people will simply list the company and the time they worked there without properly documenting their progress. The story is important, and employers want to know that you made progress in whatever job you were doing. Any time you have an opportunity to highlight an accomplishment, take advantage of it.

When you interview, be prepared to answer questions about any gaps of employment on your résumé. If you have been in the military for the past 6 years and are applying for jobs as soon as you separate, you may not need to include much from before the military. You may only need to do so if its relevant. It could raise more questions than you care to answer to list several short-lived jobs. An employer is looking for someone reliable, and gaps of employment or multiple jobs in a short time could suggest instability. However, you will likely want to include any degrees or trainings completed before the military.

The last thing I will say about résumés is to include results-oriented information that details your accomplishments in a quantifiable format. "Maintained equipment" means very little. "Supervised work section" also means very little to many hiring managers. What is more meaningful is a quantifiable result and how you got there. For example, "primarily responsible for 20-man platoon's medical equipment and care, including emergency, long-term and routine care, and maintenance of HIPAA compliant records" sounds much better than "maintained equipment."

Another example would be, "Successfully led a platoon of 43 Marines for the duration of a 9-month deployment, provided the platoon commander tactical advice that led to 8 enemy captures, directed fire during numerous firefights and successfully evacuated casualties." This sounds better than "supervised work section."

It is important to be sure that your résumé tells a story about work-related accomplishments and that it is professional and results-oriented. Take some time to survey the skills needed before creating your résumé, and be sure to get help at a career service center or from a professional résumé company if possible.

Tips:

▶ Avoid military jargon, acronyms, and terminology on your résumé.

▶ Research job descriptions in your field to glean common terms for use on your résumé.

▶ Focus on quantifiable, results-oriented information to prove your worth.

CHAPTER SEVEN
REACHING OUT

Now that you have decided on the field, have a list of possible employment opportunities, and have completed a representative résumé, it is time for you to start the application process. Be sure to build a list of point of contacts (POCs) for the various companies you are interested in. They can be hiring managers or HR representatives listed in the job posting, employees you met at career fairs, alumni who can help you better understand the company through informational interviews, or mutual professional social media connections. If the POC is directly involved with the hiring process, try to get in touch with him or her to confirm receipt of your résumé. If not, you can approach the POC with more general questions (e.g. company culture, career paths, etc.) and ask for 15 minutes from his or her busy schedules for an informational interview. Remember to research the company as well as the POC (if he or she is available) online.

Be aware of the manner in which you approach some-one. It is probably a good idea to create a LinkedIn profile for these types of interactions, because people are generally more open to and expectant of being approached with professional questions on LinkedIn versus other social media accounts. You want a potential employer to view you in a professional light, so you should behave professionally. Don't send direct messages to private profiles on Instagram or Facebook if the person is not known to you. Also, if you do reach out to a person and don't get a response, let it go. Don't follow up with more phone calls or emails.

If you do get an informational interview with a POC, be sure to prepare in advance. Research the company beforehand so that you can ask a couple of meaningful questions such as,

> ▶ I noticed that your company has locations in 35 countries around the globe. What percentage of the overall revenue of the company is derived from the location where I would be working?

> ▶ A strong training program is an important factor in my choice of company. Can you tell me a little about your program?

> ▶ I noticed that your business has continued to expand in North America over the past three years. What is the primary reason for that growth?

Questions that show employers you have taken the time to research their business and understand basic concepts can help set you apart from other candidates. You should avoid asking too many questions over the phone; however. two or three well-planned, well-placed questions may help you to stand out from other applicants.

List of Strong Questions

1. _____

2. _____

3. _____

4. _____

5. _____

6. _____

7. _____

During the call, emphasize your desire to meet with them and see if they will commit to a date to meet. The little bit of extra time spent with a POC can make a big difference. This approach can also save you some time particularly in the case where there may be an old job posting that has already been filled. Talking to someone live is almost always a good idea.

Tips:

- ▶ Building a list of Points of Contact can be a way to get an informal interview at a company you are interested in.

- ▶ If you are going to 'cold call' strangers online, use LinkedIn and avoid sending messages to accounts on other platforms whose privacy settings are set to "Private."

CHAPTER EIGHT
FACE TO FACE

ONE OF THE MOST important skills for you to master as you transition is learning to relate to and talk to civilians. Chances are, many of your friends and coworkers for the past several years were in the military. As you embark on your new life post-service, you will undoubtedly be exposed to more civilians than before.

When I first got out of the military, I became a non-traditional student at UCONN. My first semester, I sat in the back of all my classes with my Oakley's on, convinced I had nothing in common with any of the kids I shared a classroom with. As time went on, however, I slowly allowed myself to engage with the other students and my instructors. I took a class with a man whose family had survived the genocide in Rwanda. I went to summer session with a football player who ended up playing in the NFL. I had brilliant professors and small groups with other students who thoroughly impressed me academically. None of these people had been in the military, but they were interesting people who taught me things. I soon realized that my life could be as rich as it was in the military, just in a different way, if I allowed it to be.

Think about the people you served with and the vast diversity of their backgrounds. You probably had friendships or professional relationships with men and women from all over the country with vastly different backgrounds than yours. Just as you were able to get along with a number of people in the military, you will be able to find friends in the civilian world. Do not assume that because someone did not serve in the military, he or she has never done anything interesting or been of service. Talk about other things. Discuss your other interests. You will find that if you don't limit yourself to only socializing with other veterans, your horizons will broaden.

Interviews are a great opportunity to practice treating your military experience as one of your many assets instead of your identity. Although the interview process can be intimidating at first, with practice you will be excited for a chance in person to distinguish yourself from a stack of résumés. Interviewing is a skill, so like any skill, you should practice it. As you begin your job search, accept any interview you get, even for a job you don't think you'll take. This will allow you to get a feel for the interview process and gain some confidence. Interview early and often, well before you need to start actually working.

For some companies, the interview process can last several months and include several rounds of interviews, so it's a good practice to begin the process well before you actually need a job. Starting early will also allow you to be more selective with companies and offers, and it can reduce the amount of stress you feel from needing to get a job.

When you begin applying to companies, you want to apply to as many viable companies as you can, thus increasing your chances of getting multiple interviews and allowing you to develop your confidence and come across as a stronger candidate. As you start to get called for interviews, some companies may allow you to pick a time to come in. If you can, start with your least favorite options first so that you can get some extra practice during your first few interviews. This way, by the time you get to your top picks, you are well-practiced and prepared for the questions they will have for you.

Before you interview, familiarize yourself with current events, news associated with the company you are interviewing with, and the latest industry trends. Staying current will show that you are a well-rounded and knowledgeable candidate who can discuss a variety of topics. If you know anyone who has been through the same interview before, talk to him or her about what to expect. Do not underestimate the power of preparation.

Dress professionally. Some employers will notify you of the dress code for the interview. If you are not sure what something means, for example the difference between business and business casual, look it up. Ultimately, overdressed is always best to show that you are taking the interview seriously. Be sure to have a firm handshake and look everyone in the eye. Smile when you meet them and when you are leaving. It is also a good idea to brush up on basic information about the company, such as where it is headquartered, how many employees it has, how many customers it serves, and what its focus is. Interviewers commonly ask what you know about their company, and you should be prepared to answer.

An interview is your opportunity to sell yourself. It is important to be confident and enthusiastic but also to be truthful. If you are dishonest in an interview and the lie is later uncovered, it's unlikely you will be offered a job. Let the interviewer lead the interview, and don't talk too much. It is ok if there is silence at different periods of time, and it's ok to pause to consider your answers. Be prepared to discuss your experience in previous jobs and relate that experience to what you will be doing at this new job. Don't bad mouth previous employers or supervisors, use professional language and tone, and stay on topic. It is most important to come across as "human." If all of your answers sound canned, the interviewer will know that you are just accustomed to interviewing, and you won't really stand out. If you are able to tie your skills together with your experience and your interests, you will be much more memorable.

There are many types of interview, and you may not know what you're walking into until you're there. You may be interviewed by one or more people: a panel. You may be interviewed over the phone. You may even be asked to demonstrate a task. Remain calm, be courteous to everyone you encounter, and answer all questions to the best of your ability. Because you are coming from the military, it may be your default to use the terms "sir" and "ma'am." However, depending on the age of the interviewers and/or the geographic location of the interview, they may not be accustomed to being referred as "sir" or "ma'am." If you were raised in the South, simply use these terms daily, or are trying to err on the side of caution, it's never a bad idea to be respectful. However, if the interviewer requests that you stop, you should respect his/her wishes.

Although it may make you nervous, many interviews actually end up quite boring. The more genuine enthusiasm you can inject, the more likely your interviewer will remember you. While you don't want to come across as hyper or jittery, if you can connect with your interviewer, you have a better chance of making a lasting impression.

It is impossible to know exactly what you will be asked in an interview, but you should be prepared to demonstrate your knowledge of the company, knowledge of the job, and be able to discuss your past employment. Interviewers also often ask about your personality and ability to work with others on a team and your strengths and weaknesses. Think about what you might say on these topics, considering what we already discussed about fit. Of course, you don't want to admit to a prospective employer that you despise working with others on a daily basis, but if an interviewer repeatedly stresses that teamwork is vital to company culture, you might consider that the job is not a great fit for you.

The typical types of questions an interviewer will ask in a non-technical interview should fit into one of a few categories. While this list is in no way comprehensive, we will cover a few common question-types and examples. In addition to the questions below, before each interview think about other questions you may be asked. If the interview is for a technical position or a field in which you are an expert, expect questions that cover the technical elements of your specific field of expertise.

Question Types

Opening Questions: These questions open the interview and are designed to "break the ice." There is no wrong answer to these questions, so don't worry too much about your answer – just act natural and conversational.

▸ How was the traffic on the way here?

▸ How is the weather outside today?

▸ Did you see what the market did this morning?

▸ Have you been following the ____ in the news?

Tip: The morning/day of the interview, take some time for final preparations. Review the company's website one more time, look up the interviewers' professional social media and any social media where they are quoted, and familiarize yourself with any industry news or developments.

If you feel comfortable and calm when you walk in to the interview, you will more likely have a good interview.

It's also a good idea to familiarize yourself with national and global current events and general local news. If the interviewer asks you questions about what's going on in the news, you don't want to be completely oblivious or seem out of touch with your community. The last thing you want is for an interviewer to assume you are a completely one-dimensional veteran.

If you are asked about a topic that you are not familiar with, don't fake it. Just let the interviewer know that you aren't familiar with the subject and move on.

One area where you may find you have an advantage over your civilian counterparts is your ability to follow a schedule. Having been in the military, you should understand the importance of punctuality. It remains important once you leave the military. Be on time for your interview. Be sure you know of the location the night before, and account for traffic the day of. As we said in the SEAL Teams, "Plan your dive and dive your plan."

Transition Questions: These questions are designed as a segue to the more focused questions throughout the rest of the interview.

► How did you hear about the job opening?

► Tell us what you know about our company?

▶ What interests you about working here?

▶ What makes you an ideal candidate for this job?

▶ Did anyone discuss with you in detail the responsibilities of the job we are looking to fill?

Tip: Some of the questions about the company you will have answered by doing your pre- interview research, but be sure to take a second look at the job description before the interview. After re-reading the job description, think about why you are a good candidate for the job and how your experience specifically relates to this job. You may want to print out the job description and list out the reasons you are a great candidate next to each requirement.

If you have an initial phone interview prior to the actual face-to-face interview, ask the caller for a detailed description of the job and ask them to explain the daily responsibilities. You can also ask phone interviewers to describe their "perfect candidate." Having someone answer these questions for you ahead of time will allow you to better organize your thoughts for the Transition Questions.

Experience/ Basic Knowledge: These questions focus on skill sets and basic knowledge as well as employment experience.

▶ Walk me through your résumé.

▶ Tell me about your role and responsibilities in your last job.

▶ Tell me about your computer and software knowledge.

▶ What experience do you have in the field of _____?

▶ How do your studies relate to this position?

▶ With very little experience in our industry, what skills can you bring to this new role that will help you to be successful?

Tip: You already took the time to write an impactful résumé which helped to get you the face-to-face interview. Be sure that you take some time to practice verbalizing the answers to these questions. This is your opportunity to present your value to the company in person, so your answers need to be clear and concise. Remember to directly relate your experience and achievements to the requirements of the new position. Just like you did on the résumé, describe the results you achieved in your previous jobs and communicate how the same skills can help you to be successful in this new role.

Behavioral Questions and Teamwork: The goal of these questions is to understand how you will deal with basic instruction, stress, adversity, feedback, etc.

▶ Tell me about a time when you had a tough personnel issue that you were able to resolve.

▶ Tell me about your favorite job, and why you liked it.

▶ Tell me about your least favorite job, and why you disliked it.

▶ Tell me about a conflict with another soldier, what happened, and how you resolved it.

▶ Tell me about a time when you helped improve a process within your platoon, and what prompted you to come up with this solution?

▶ Tell me about a time when you managed a team that was successful and what you did to ensure success.

▶ Tell me about a time when you were a part of a team that was unsuccessful. Why were they unsuccessful, and what did you learn from the experience?

Tip: Now that you understand the goal of the Behavioral Questions, pick some stories from your previous experiences where you demonstrated strong qualities that had a positive impact on your job performance. If you are newer to the job market and have only military experience, use examples from the military. The hiring manager saw your résumé and will be expecting you to use mostly examples from your time in the military.

Keep your answers clear, concise, positive, and results-oriented. Focus on the facts and not the emotion, particularly if you are describing a conflict situation that you were able to resolve. Remember the focus of these questions is to help the interviewer better understand your capabilities to overcome obstacles and turn negative situations into positive situations. Make sure that your examples demonstrate these abilities.

Strengths and Weaknesses: These questions are designed to discover your strengths and weaknesses.

▶ Tell me your top three strengths.

▶ Tell me your top three weaknesses.

▶ How will these strengths factor into this new role?

▶ How might the weaknesses prevent your success in this role?

▶ What skill improvements will you need to make if you are hired into this role?

▶ What skills do you possess that will help you to be successful in this role?

Tip: Many people struggle with Strength and Weakness questions. Everyone has strengths and weaknesses. A single attribute can be either a strength or a weakness, depending on the specifics of a given situation. In other words, your strengths are also your weaknesses.

Think about your strengths and why they will help you to be successful in the new position. Then consider what situations might cause each strength you identified to become a weakness.

For example, being outgoing and helpful could be a strength in a job where you deal with customers every day. But being too outgoing and too helpful might mean that it takes you longer to complete certain tasks.

Similarly, being thorough and detail oriented could be a strength in a job where you analyze information, but it could also be a weakness if you spend too much time on a single detail or assignment.

By understanding your strengths, you can better articulate your weaknesses. Again, be sure that your answers are clear and concise. Practice answering these types of questions before the interview so that you are comfortable discussing your strengths and weaknesses in a straightforward way. You should be able to explain why your strengths are valuable to the new position but also demonstrate that you understand how to minimize the impact of your weaknesses.

Be honest with the employer and yourself about your strengths and weaknesses. Remember, you don't want to just "win the job." You want to be in a situation where you enjoy your job and build a platform for a strong, continued career growth.

Brain Teasers: Some companies use brain teasers to understand your ability to problem solve, ask questions, think on your feet, and make recommendations.

▸ How many phone calls are made in the city of Boston per month?

▶ How many golf balls would fit into a in a green plastic trash can?

▶ How much dog food is used by the residents of this county on an annual basis?

Tip: First and foremost, remember the interviewer is primarily interested in your thought process and how you arrive at the answer. Take a minute to collect your thoughts, and be sure that you understand the question. Feel free to ask any pertinent clarifying questions.

Start with the macro elements first, and then drill down to the micro elements. For instance, you probably need to estimate the number of households in Boston first in order to begin to determine the number of phone calls made in the city per month.

If needed, take out your notebook, and write down the question. Begin listing the pertinent information included in the question and the steps you would take to arrive at the correct answer. Remember, the interviewer doesn't want the exact numerical answer to the question. He or she simply wants to better understand your process and the steps you will take to arrive at an answer.

To answer the question, simply walk the interviewer through the process you would use to solve the problem.

Getting-to-Know-You Questions: These questions are used to learn more about you and how you think.

► What is the last book you read?

► What is the best word to describe you?

► What do you like to do in your free time?

Tip: For these questions, the interviewer wants to get to know who you are, so don't answer to impress. Answer honestly, and be ready to describe the reasons.

Employee Expectations: These questions are designed to help the employer understand your expectations of the company and your new role.

► What are you looking for in a new company?

What interests you most about this new role?

► Where do you see yourself in three years?

► What kind of training would you like to see us put into place?

► What other companies are you interviewing with?

► What questions do you have for us?

► What are your salary expectations?

► How soon can you start?

Tip: Understand what you are really looking for in a new career and company so that you can discuss it with the interviewer and assess whether the opportunity is right for you. Before the interview, write down questions you want the employer to answer and be ready to talk about your vision for your career and future. Consider your salary expectations and when you will be available to start your new job. Do some research ahead of time to see what the average salary for this type of job is. Coming out of the military, you might not have a good idea of what to expect. You don't want to look ridiculous by telling a hiring manager that your expectation is $165,000 salary when the average pay is $75,000. Taking the time to detail these answers before the interview will help to expedite the process and ensure that you can effectively evaluate options.

Unexpected Questions: Because of the spontaneous nature of interviews, you won't know everything that is going to be asked.

If you are surprised by a random question and are not sure how to answer, stay calm and answer honestly. If you need a little time to collect your thoughts, you can ask a clarifying question, ask the interviewer to repeat the question or simply repeat the question back to the interviewer before answering. Try to avoid using stall words to fill the space like "uh" or "um." Just let the silence fill the space. Silence is fine during an interview, so you should get used to it. If you often use fill words, you can practice with a friend, family member, peer, or acquaintance in a mock interview.

As mentioned previously, this list is in no way comprehensive, but it should give you a sense of possible question types and help you to think through how your experience, qualifications, and other skill sets relate to the new role.

As you work through pre-interview questions and prepare for your first interview, you can get some great practice by answering questions with a friend or family member. Just as you trained for real world situations in the military, it's a smart idea to train for your real interview. For this exercise, you can give the practice questions to your friend of family member and let him or her ask you the questions in any order he or she wants. This will help you become more comfortable before the actual interview. It's important to practice and hear yourself answer the questions so that you can get comfortable with the process. This way, if you struggle with any of the questions or feel like the answers sound unclear or disorganized, you can adjust before the actual interview.

As you build your confidence and get more comfortable with the process, let your practice interviewer add his or her own questions and follow-ups to your responses. This will add some variety and spontaneity to better replicate the actual interview process while you practice.

Once you begin your real interviews with real companies, you should jot down the interview questions. Make note of the questions that were asked of you that you didn't expect and those that were tough to answer. You will be interviewing with multiple companies while you narrow down your choices, and keeping these questions will help you to better prepare for your next interview.

Some companies will require you to interview with multiple people separately and may ask for several follow-up interviews as they narrow their candidate choices. Taking notes during or immediately after each interview can be particularly helpful because companies that use multiple interviews and interviewers may ask the same or very similar questions.

Tips:

- ▶ Begin interviewing as soon as possible, and take every interview you are offered so that you can develop your interviewing skills.

- ▶ Prepare for interviews by practicing with a friend/family member.

- ▶ Pay special attention to preparing the strengths/weaknesses questions.

CHAPTER NINE

CONNECTING

NOW THAT YOU ARE aware of the types of interview questions, it is important that you understand how to effectively connect with an interviewer. "Connecting" begins when two people truly understand each other's viewpoint. It is the first step in building trust and eventually creates mutual understanding. You have probably experienced what it's like to connect at different points in your life. Maybe this happened in a conversation with a friend or family member while trying to solve a problem. The moment when you and the other person suddenly understood each other, you were connecting.

Connecting is critically important during any conversation where you need to reach a decision. An interview is a place where you need to connect with the interviewer so that you can understand what he or she is looking for and he or she can understand what you are looking for. The first step to connecting is to listen. Let the other person talk, and be sure that you understand exactly what he or she is asking. Don't interrupt, but if you are even a little unclear, pause for a moment and then ask a clarifying question. Asking questions shows the person that you are listening and genuinely interested in answering the question he or she asked. In the military, you may have had experiences when you felt it was appropriate to maintain silence while you were "talked at" by a superior. An interview in the civilian world is not one of those situations. You must listen, engage, and respond.

The second step is to provide adequate information. After answering a question, look for signs that the interviewer is satisfied with the type of response you gave. It is very possible that the phrasing of the question he or she asked meant one thing to the interviewer and a completely different thing to you. When this happens, you and the interviewer move further from mutual understanding, the interviewer won't get the information he or she is seeking, and you may miss an opportunity to demonstrate your value. If you are not sure how to interpret the interviewer's reaction, simply ask, "Does that answer the question?" or "Does that make sense?" By doing so you can be sure that the interviewer got the type of response he or she was looking for. If there was a miscommunication, it will give the interviewer an opportunity to rephrase the question.

Step three: be interesting. Step back from the canned answers, and give some context to who you really are. Canned answers are boring and push you and the interviewer further from connecting. Think about the interests you have, and relate them to the job you are applying for. If you like sports, music, or the outdoors, talk about why your experiences in those areas make you a stronger fit for the company. For example, I played rugby in college. If I were applying for a job where teamwork was important, I could reference a situation where through teamwork we were able to pull out a second half win. It's also important to establish yourself as a three-dimensional person, not just a veteran. Sure, you should use your military experience, when appropriate, to answer questions and relate to the job, but try to stretch and think of your other interests and experiences, as well. You want the interviewer to remember *you*, and not just that you wore a uniform. You can make this distinction in the interviewer's mind if you talk about more than your military experience.

Interests You Have That Relate to the Job and Why?

1. _____

2. _____

3. _____

4. _____

5. _____

6. _____

7. _____

In situations where an interviewee has little work experience, these kinds of "interest related" experiences give the interviewer something he or she can work with. The interviewer could then ask:

▶ "How did you get the team to pull together?"

▶ "Did you like the leadership style of your coach, why or why not?"

▶ "What do you think led to your success that time?"

Positioning interests puts you in a "human" context, adds depth to you as a potential employee, and grants the employer options for questions to assess fit.

As we discussed in the last chapter, during the interview, employers will ask you for any questions that you may have. This is an opportunity for you to further connect and ask questions that give you a clearer picture of what you are getting into with this new company. The questions you prepared before the interview can also be used to highlight some of the things you learned about the company during your research. You should also note questions that you develop during the interview so that you can ask about them later. Try to ask at least one question. If they ask you for your questions and you don't have any, it may appear that you are not really interested. Preparing questions shows the interviewer that you take the process seriously. A few examples of this are:

▶ "I noticed that the company's growth last year was 15 percent. How did this market compare to the national growth?"

▶ "You mentioned a training program. Can you tell me a little more about that?"

▶ "What does a typical day look like for someone in this position?"

▶ How does this role help to support the overall vision of the business?

Questions like these will help you get a better understanding of the position and also show the interviewer that you have done your homework, listened to what he or she said during the interview, and have a genuine interest in making the right decision, not just "winning the job."

Questions for the Interview

1. _____

2. _____

3. _____

4. _____

5. _____

Be sure to follow up after the interview. It is fine to write an email to employers thanking them for the opportunity to interview; however, a hand written thank you note can be a great way to differentiate you from other candidates. You may want to incorporate relevant topics that you discussed with the interviewer to personalize your thank you note.

CHAPTER TEN
SO MANY OPTIONS

Now that you understand the interviewing process, you should interview with as many companies as possible. There are a few advantages when you successfully interview with several companies. One obvious advantage is that you receive multiple job offers. Receiving more offers provides more choices, and with more choices, you may gain some negotiating leverage. The biggest overall advantage to fielding multiple offers is that it gives you an opportunity to look more closely at each opportunity and choose the one that is right for you. There are some basics steps that you should take when dealing with multiple offers in order to ensure that you are fair to each company while you are determining your top pick.

Step One: Thank each potential employer for the opportunity and offer. You need to be genuine in your appreciation. It is a lot of work for a company to conduct interviews, weigh candidate options, put together an offer, and get all the approvals and paperwork done.

Step Two: Ask the employer for some time to make your decision. You should reiterate your excitement about the opportunity, but let them know that there are several companies who have made offers and you want to ensure that you make the right choice. They may ask what others are offering you. Answering generically is a good approach. You could say something like, "Each company has provided a very competitive offer, but I need to look more closely at the specifics of each."

Step Three: If the employer says, "Okay. I understand that this is a big decision. Let us know by next week what you decide," then you can thank them and move on. However, if the employer asks, "What will it take to get you to sign with us right now?" you have a choice; you can give them an answer and make a decision, or you can stall them. To stall, simply say, "I really want to make sure I evaluate everything. I will call you next week and let you know where I stand." The employer may still press you for an immediate decision. If pressed, you can simply revert to your previous statement and ask for a little time. Some employers want to quickly weed through candidates so that they don't get stuck waiting a few weeks only to find that the candidate will choose another company. By then, many of the other top candidates the company interviewed may have moved on, and the company might have to start the process all over again. Most companies will give you a little extra time to decide, but the top companies won't wait around long because they have a strong pool of candidates who want to work for them.

Step Four: Look back at your company and job list and compare your options. You should examine the attributes of each opportunity: your overall career path, the company's financial strength, its corporate culture, your job function, compensation, benefits, location, and of course, any other areas that are important to your decision. Evaluating which company to choose is the fun part.

Step Five: Create a chart with the companies at the top and the attributes down the left side. Mark each of the companies that have the things that you want and rank the companies from first place to last place.

Chart of Offers and Attributes

Company:	1.	2.	3.
Attribute			
Attribute			
Attribute			
Attribute			
Attribute			
Attribute			

Now, call the top company first and begin your negotiations. You want to choose the top company first because unlike in the interview process where you have a lot of time to develop and get comfortable, the negotiation process is time sensitive. The top companies are likely interviewing many other capable candidates who like the company and may accept any offer the company extends to them. You need your top company to know how interested you are immediately. If they don't hear from you for several days, they may just move on to their next top choice.

It's not out of the realm of possibility that you reach an agreement with your top choice after a phone call. If the top company is not your first phone call, you may unfairly prevent the other companies who extended offers to you from moving on to extend offers to other candidates. It is a simple courtesy to allow the companies you do not intend to choose to move on and offer other candidates the job.

Step Six: Fielding multiple offers. The act of negotiating may be new to you if this is your first job outside of the military. In the military, your salary and special pays were based on the amount of time you'd been in the service and where you were stationed and were non-negotiable. Depending on where you are interviewing, you may have some room to negotiate your pay or hiring package.

You don't want to lead companies on, and this is a time sensitive process. Ultimately, you will likely have to sacrifice some things for other things regardless of the company that you choose. Decide what is most important, and call the first company. Explain that you really appreciate the opportunity and you would like to sign with them, but you need them to look at a few items. The items could be salary, stock, stock options, retirement contribution, signing bonus, continued education, etc. If they tell you that they have no room to negotiate, then you may want to tell them that you will have a decision for them after you speak with the other companies. Be sure to thank them again for the opportunity, and then move to the next company on the list. If they say that they will take a look at the items and get back to you, then ask for a date and time when you will talk again.

Try to negotiate down the list one at a time. It may seem like a good idea to pit every company against each other and see who comes back with the best offer, but that can put you in a position where you burn bridges in the industry where you will be working. Remember that today people are more professionally transient than they were 50 years ago, and you never know who you may end up interviewing with again or who could be hired on in the future to work with or above you. The best approach is to try first to reach a win-win with the top company on your list because you are both interested in reaching an agreement and you have both determined that there is a good fit. If the top company won't negotiate, you can either accept their terms or move on to your next choice.

Step Seven: Choose the company that makes the most sense. Sign the offer letter, and make sure that the deal is done. Tell your new employer that you will inform the other companies that you have made a decision. Once the deal is secure, tell the other companies of your decision, and thank them for the opportunity and the time they put into the process. If you are professional and grateful, many of the companies may offer to stay in touch with you in case you ever decide to make a move.

Step Eight: Fill out the paperwork with your new company, and spend a little time talking with the hiring manager to begin an open dialogue. You will want to confirm your first day, your training schedule, dress attire, and what materials to bring. While you are talking with the new manager, ask him or her about the company's vision and how your role will help accomplish the vision. This not only gives you insight into the company's vision, but it will also solidify in the manager's mind the value of your role and remind him or her why attention to your training is critical to the company's overall success. It is important to get a lot of support in your new role. By asking what your role is, you seem ready to be a team player and you don't accidentally appear arrogant.

Tips:

▶ As you attempt to negotiate and accept an offer, stick to the timelines you and your prospective employers agree upon.

▶ Maintain communication with anyone who makes an offer, even if it's to politely decline.

▶ Research offers and realistic expectations to aid in your negotiations.

CHAPTER ELEVEN

FIRST, SECOND, AND THIRD IMPRESSIONS

GETTING HIRED AT A new job outside of the military is a big step in your transition process. As you continue your journey, there are still several things to consider. The next several chapters are designed to help acclimate you to your new civilian environment and help you create plans to succeed in your new life and career.

As you begin your new career, every day will provide you the opportunity to add value to your personal brand. Adding value to your brand will help you with the tangible elements of your career such as promotions, salary negotiation, and opportunities for growth within your field.

From the moment you show up on your first day at your new job, people will begin to categorize you. As the old saying goes, "You only get one chance to make a first impression." If you appear arrogant, shy, loud, or silly, then that will be the way you are viewed in the office for a while. Similarly, if you come off as the guy who talks about nothing but being in the military, that's how you'll be known. Realize that everyone makes judgements about other people, and they will be judging you the moment you walk through the door on the first day. Your co-workers may lose interest in you if you constantly refer to your time in the service. Conversely, your personal brand value will increase significantly through your positive contributions on the job rather than your references to things you did years ago.

It's important to understand that your status as a veteran will automatically earn you a certain amount of respect from many of your coworkers, but many of them will also feel uncomfortable asking about your military experience or unsure of how to approach you. Realize that just as adjusting to your new life is a learning process for you, making friends or working with a veteran can also be a learning process for some of your coworkers. In my experience, many people with no military experience worry they will say the wrong thing or will not show enough deference, which can make connecting difficult. They often assume it's a bigger deal than it actually is. The more on task you are at work and willing to contribute to the product, the more likely your coworkers will see you as one of them and more than just a label.

Remember to be polite, enthusiastic, helpful, and appreciative of everyone you meet regardless of his or her title, position, etc. You never know who the true influencers are in a new job.

In most jobs, you should expect some training. Similar to the military, it is important to take training seriously and master all material you are presented with. Be sure you understand all of the information you are receiving. Ask questions of the trainer and other employees when needed, but try not to overburden the employees around you. While you are training, there is very little to measure your success other than your ability to learn. Since many companies have a lot of individual online training now, it is important to periodically update your manager on your success. You should schedule a little time each week to discuss your progress with your training staff and/or manager. By taking the initiative to set the meetings, you will show the employer that you are a self-starter and that you take the training seriously. The update will also give you an opportunity to "connect" with your supervisor and understand what is most important to him or her. Some managers may not have time each week, but simply suggesting the meeting will differentiate you from other trainees.

Tips:

► Prepare to be judged on your appearance and behavior immediately upon starting your new job.

► In the same way that most veterans feel they don't relate to civilians, many civilians struggle with how to talk to veterans. You can address this with your coworkers by staying task oriented, but you can also open up about your interests and hobbies and find things you have in common. Keep an open mind about those around you.

CHAPTER TWELVE
PLANNING FOR SUCCESS

Putting together a plan for your career is very important to a smooth and successful transition. When you have a documented career plan rather than a few thoughts in your head, you will have a much clearer path to track your progress and plan your success. When I speak to corporate groups, I refer to "hitting the 5-meter target, then the 10-meter target, and then the 20-meter target." Set short term and long-term goals for yourself now. Throughout your new career, you will be able to refer to the plan and add new details.

As you contemplate how to attain success throughout your transition, consider both personal and professional goals. True, the major aspect of your life that is changing is your job, but yours is a career that has impacted your personal life in many ways. A life in the military means a certain lifestyle, and much of that will change as you enter civilian life. Take a look back at the questions you answered in the first section of the book about your goals.

▶ Write down long- and short-term goals.

A. _____

B. _____

C. _____

D. _____

E. _____

▶ Write down the big picture things that will need to happen for you to accomplish your goals.

A. _____

B. _____

C. _____

D. _____

E. _____

▶ Now consider the specific steps you will need to take to accomplish those goals.

A. _____

B. _____

C. _____

D. _____

E. _____

▶ Once you understand the steps, add in timelines for completion.

A. _____

B. _____

C. _____

D. _____

E. _____

▶ Add in what you will need to do this year, month, week, and day to meet your goals.

A. _____

B. _____

C. _____

D. _____

E. _____

▶ Now list the items that may prevent you from accomplishing these goals.

A. _____

B. _____

C. _____

D. _____

E. _____

▶ Think about what additional steps you could take to ensure successful completion of your goals.

A. _____

B. _____

C. _____

D. _____

E. _____

Now you should have a road map of what you will need to accomplish each day to successfully transition and reach your goals. Realize that these lists are not set in stone and that you can update, adjust, and modify them at any time as your goals or timelines change. That way your timeline evolves as your career evolves.

Once your goal planning is done, you should put together a daily tasking list. This list will be based on your daily goals and include the specific actions that you will need to accomplish in order to achieve your daily goals. The daily task list will have "to do" items that can be added or crossed off each day.

Daily Task List:

A. _____

B. _____

C. _____

D. _____

E. _____

Tips:

▶ Set your short term and long-term goals now. Revise them as necessary.

CHAPTER THIRTEEN
EXECUTION

Now THAT YOU HAVE a plan in place, you need to execute the plan. Execution will make the difference in your success or failure. Every day, you will move closer to or further from accomplishing your overall goals. If you work harder and smarter, you will move closer. Here are a few tips to keep in mind when working toward building a successful transition.

▶ Stay on task, and focus on mastering your new job. Measure your own performance each day, and don't waste time. Think about the goals of the organization and your own personal goals, and be sure you are spending time on things that make progress toward these goals. It is easy to get sidetracked by something that is "quasi" important or something that is more "fun" but is of little value. For example, don't be the professional veteran spending hours per day building his social media following if your career doesn't rely on something you market online. It could be argued that online engagement could lead to networking, but likes on Instagram rarely directly translate to cash in the bank. Unless your job is to sell things online, your time is better spent focusing on the task at hand with revenue generating customers.

▶ Always learn everything you can. Continued learning should occur for the rest of your life if you want to become truly successful. Just as training never ended in the military, you will need to continue to better yourself to stay relevant in your new career. Depending on the company, there may be online learning modules, webinars, or classes available to you that you can assign yourself and take at your convenience. It is important to always evaluate your own learning needs and not wait for someone else to tell you what to do. Ask about additional opportunities that the company offers for continuing education. A top performer with a great command of information can be very valuable to any company, so be sure to take the initiative.

▶ Work on building professional relationships with others. While achieving your own goals, lend a hand to help others accomplish their goals. You should always keep your eye on your own performance and be sure that you achieve your own goals, but developing a strong network of teammates can multiply your ability to achieve. Internal and external resources can add a lot of value through collaborative goal achievement, so understand the motivations and needs of your teammates, and offer help when you can. You have the advantage of military service where you likely worked with a diverse group of people. You may be asked to work with people who have less life experience than you, who annoy you, or whose beliefs differ dramatically from yours. You've already proven you can work with anyone, and being able to maintain a professional attitude is a valuable skill to bring from the military to the civilian world.

▶ Be Punctual. Tardiness may give the impression that you don't care. If you plan to be fifteen minutes early always, you will rarely be late. Meetings, training, events, etc. are opportunities to interact with others and develop your skills and career, so arrive early so that you have a little time to socialize before the event begins. If you are early to the office, you may get some time to learn something new, reflect on the day, or just collect your thoughts before work.

▶ Be Responsive. Unresponsiveness can often be perceived as a lack of interest or initiative. Return calls and emails quickly. If you don't have an answer but you plan to work on getting the answer, return the call and explain. If you don't return the call, the other person may feel like you are ignoring him/her or that you are unreliable. When you have a lot of emails or phone calls to return, take a second and prioritize. Respond to the most urgent, important communications first, and then respond to the others. Twenty-four hours may be acceptable for less urgent responses, but in many cases, people expect an answer within a couple of hours or less. Be sure to stay on top of communication. It makes a big difference.

- ► Make good choices. Remember, building a successful career is a long-term process. Making a snap decision that lacks thought is a bad idea. Think through the long-term effects of each decision, and don't burn bridges unnecessarily. Making solid, big picture decisions will help you to achieve long-term success.

- ► Reflect. Becoming truly effective at building a successful career requires time for reflection each day. Think about your progress toward reaching your goals. Consider what you may need to do differently, and make the appropriate changes to your plan and task list. Daily reflection will allow you to make appropriate modifications as needed to reach your goals.

- ► Spend time each day learning about the field you are in. Read articles, blogs, and trade magazines to stay in the know. You should be able to reference material you have read when talking with others in your industry. If you take your career seriously, others will too.

- ► Ask for feedback. You can create a healthy dialogue with your manager, team members, employees, and internal and external resources by asking for regular feedback. Be sure to listen and make the appropriate adjustments.

By doing so, you can dramatically increase your overall effectiveness and reach within the organization.

Staying out of the fray is important. You don't want to get sidetracked with things that hamper your ability to reach your goals. A few tips for in and out of the office include:

- Politics. Stay out of the politics of the office. Don't gossip, stand around and listen to gossip, or make fun of others in the office.

- Jokes. Avoid jokes that could be perceived even remotely as insulting to anyone in or out of the office. There is specific compliance information that your company should give you about employee interaction and what is and isn't appropriate and legal in the workplace. Inappropriate jokes are not only in bad taste, but they can lead to you being disciplined, fired, or even sued.

- Avoid personal relationships in the office. It is important to remember that the people you work with are not the same as your longtime friends from home or school. People may circulate personal information about you if given the opportunity, and many employees may see you as competition in the office and would take any available opportunity to get ahead. Be sure not to reveal any information in the office that you don't want everyone in the office to know. Regardless of how well you think you know a colleague, he or she probably knows someone else better, so keep your important personal information close. This may be a difficult adjustment to make coming out of the military as you likely spent so much time with some coworkers that they felt like family. You also probably trusted them with your life. Before starting your new job, realize that you won't be as close to your coworkers as you were to your peers in the military, but also that the same relationships won't be necessary.

► Keep an upbeat attitude. It is important to always be upbeat and display a great attitude while working. If you appear to be down at work often, people may wrongly believe that you are upset about work or that you are unhappy with your new job. Maintain a cheery demeanor whenever possible.

► Be enthusiastic. You should be enthusiastic about the company and your new opportunity regardless of with whom you are speaking. Customers, vendors, other divisions, and even friends may be connected in some way to people at your new job. Be sure to display enthusiasm so that your new employer is constantly reminded of your positive energy.

► Don't post negative information about work on social media. Social media can be a great tool for meeting people and making new connections, but you should expect anything you post online to be seen by others. It is a good idea to avoid posting negative info about work on your pages. If there is something that really bothers you, you may want to find another job where you will be happy.

▶ Dress professionally. Dressing professionally is important in the office. Don't wear clothing that is inappropriate for your environment. You should look at what the dress policy is at work and follow it. If you want to dress a little nicer than the minimum requirement, don't overdo it because you will seem like you are trying too hard and this may disconnect you from your colleagues. You have probably been wearing uniforms to work for the last several years and may not own a lot of civilian clothes appropriate for work. Go shopping if this is the case. Don't show up in clothes you bought 15 years ago.

▶ Happy hours. Happy hours are simply offsite employee functions. If you attend these functions, stay professional just as you would in the office. Keep in mind that many company policies and laws on harassment apply to offsite employee functions. Try not to stay too long at these functions, and don't engage in gossip before, during, or after the function.

▶ Congratulate others on their successes. Be sure to take a minute to congratulate others when they are successful. It shows that you care and will help you to develop a better rapport with teammates.

► Don't publicly discuss other people's failures. Regardless of the situation, nothing good comes out of being vocal about someone's failure. If you must give someone negative feedback, do it one-on-one, privately.

► Remember that while you are actively moving forward into the civilian world, you will always be a steward of the United States Military. You may be the first veteran of the Army/Navy/Air Force/Marine Corps/Coast Guard that someone meets. Conduct yourself in a manner that reflects positively on the service.

The big takeaway from this section is to stay focused on achieving your goals. Once you have a plan and task list completed, execute your plan. Continue to reflect, reevaluate, and always keep learning.

Tips:

► Focus on how you can keep working towards your goals every day and don't get sidetracked by things that seem fun but are less productive.

► Read your company's handbook or Human Resources materials so that you are aware of all policies. You will be responsible for them.

CHAPTER FOURTEEN

SELLING GREAT IDEAS

IT'S IMPORTANT FOR YOU to understand, regardless of which career you choose after you leave the military, that you have much more control over yourself and your career than you did previously. If you are assertive, this can be a huge advantage. If you are a person who thrived in an environment where everything was planned out for you, including your opportunities for advancement, it may take you some time to adjust to a world where selling yourself is part of getting ahead. In the military, rank and chain of command often dictated position. Out in the civilian world, merit is often given to those with the most enthusiasm and the best ideas, regardless of time on the job or age.

As you move further into your civilian career, you will need to sell in some capacity. Selling ideas to other employees, managers, and internal and external resources is a big part of any professional's job. It's important to understand the process and what is truly important to each conversation. We will cover some common scenarios and examples to illustrate the right and wrong way to sell. Listening, connecting, and reaching a clear and mutual understanding is as critical here as it was during the interviewing process.

As you get further into your career, you will develop improvement ideas. These ideas often can be very helpful to a business, but they must be presented in a way that helps others connect with the value of the idea. Some people tend to get excited about an idea and talk for a long time about the value of the idea. The problem is that most people listening have a short attention span and will lose interest in listening after about 30 seconds. When this happens, your great points will be lost because your audience will tune you out and think about whatever they want for a few minutes until you are done talking. Here is an example of the first approach:

Ask a question: "Why are we unable to hire another account manager to help us sell more into our account base and increase our business this year?"

Listen to the answer: "The current account managers can handle what we have, and we don't really need the added stress of hiring new...."

Launch into the solution: "I think we could get it all done if we really spent some time to get the right person for the job. I could find someone and hire them. That way you could avoid the stress of hiring. I have lots of experience finding good people, and my experience and contacts will really help us to locate the right person. You really should let me put this together for you since it will help the company meet its goals and allow us to grow our business. I think we could have this person really make a difference in the company, and it would be great!"

"Not right now. There are too many problems with it."

Launch right back into it: "But I think that if you just give me a chance to find the right person, we will really be able to get someone that makes all of us more successful and..."

At this point, the person you are talking to is thinking about what they need to pick up for dinner after work and what series they've been meaning to binge watch. They may be pretending to check emails, or they may even get a call they need to take.

In sales, this is called the "show up and throw up approach." It is what happens when you try to simply "tell" your ideas and force the other person to say, yes. Saying yes should not be the goal. The goal should be to reach a mutual understanding of the situation, issue, and solution, and then move forward with a resolution.

One simple principle of sales is that you must "listen and ask questions" for most of the conversation. It seems counterintuitive to listen and ask questions rather than talk, but remember the goal of the conversation. To reach mutual understanding, you must truly understand the other person, his or her obstacles, and his or her ideas on resolution. To do this you need to listen.

Often the person you are talking with doesn't really understand the situation because he or she hasn't had time to think it through. That means that the person needs to actually consider the situation, and this is why questions are much more effective than statements.

You both must completely understand the situation and obstacles before you can offer a solution. If you create a mutual understanding, then you will both develop a desire to reach a solution together. If your idea is a good one, that solves all of the issues, the other person will be much more apt to agree to your idea.

To effectively "sell" your ideas, you need to apply some basic sales concepts to your process. Here is what a basic process for selling should look like. Here is the same situation as above with a very different result:

Ask a question: "Why are we unable to hire another account manager to help us sell more into our account base and increase our business this year?"

Listen to the answer: "The current account managers can handle what we have, and we don't really need the added stress of hiring new people. Plus, the new account managers would probably be expensive, and the existing account managers would be mad if they had to give up accounts."

Repeat the key points: "Ok, so it would be stressful to hire someone new, they would be expensive, and our existing account managers would not want to give up accounts." Check for a mutual understanding: "Is that right?"

"Yes. That's right."

Ask about the effect of non-resolution: "What will happen if we don't grow our business this year?"

"We will probably have to cut two positions."

Repeat the effect: "So, we will lose two positions?"
"Yes"

Ask about the options: "What options do we have to increase revenues?"

"We need to get our people selling more into the existing accounts, and we need them to generate new business development. We have a headcount to add a person, but I am afraid we won't grow, and then we will need to cut three people."

Repeat the key options: "So, we need to sell to existing and new business accounts, and we have a headcount to hire another person?" Ask about your idea: "What if I found a new business development person instead of an account manager for a reasonable price, and they only sold to incremental new business accounts?"

Listen: "Well that might work, but no one is going to be affordable and only want to work on new accounts."

Ask clarifying questions: "What is affordable for us right now?"

"X thousand per year."

State your solution idea: "I would like the opportunity to find a person who will work for less than X thousand per year who is solely focused on new business."

Listen to concerns: "Who will train them?"

Ask for the opportunity to work toward reaching an agreement: "I will find this person and let you interview them. Then, I can train them if you will agree to use the open headcount."

"Fine, if you find and train them, I will get the headcount."

This approach allows both of you to reach a solution together. The manager may not be completely convinced that the approach will work, but he or she wants to find a solution. Fully aware of the situation and what will happen to the business if a solution is not found to the issue, the manager looks to you for help. This approach has made finding the right solution a joint effort rather than something that only one person is committed to.

Tips:

- ► Get comfortable with the idea of more autonomy and influence through selling than you had in the military.

- ► Learn to listen and ask questions when selling an idea.

CHAPTER FIFTEEN
SELLING YOURSELF

SELLING YOURSELF IS A little different than selling your ideas. In the military, certain things were already figured out for you that may benefit you in your civilian career. You don't want to come across as a shameless self-promoter, but it's important to be aware of the situations that may call for you to show some initiative and sell yourself in order to better your position:

▸ Selling one-on-one for a raise: Although careers exist outside of the military where salary or pay is fixed on steps, you may be starting a job where your pay and future raises are negotiable. If this is the case, you may one day find yourself in a one-on-one conversation with your manager, selling yourself for a raise. Treat this conversation as a negotiation. Your leverage is that you can always leave, and their leverage is that they believe you won't leave. The important thing to remember about leverage is that it's only effective if used correctly. If you come right out and threaten to leave, you need to be prepared to walk out the door and collect your things because your manager may call your bluff and ask you to go. That's why a better approach is to understand what your manager expects of you before you walk into the negotiation. If you are conducting the weekly or bi-weekly meetings with your manager, you should have a good sense of expectations. Before you walk into the meeting, prepare notes and figures on everything you have done that has exceeded expectations. Prepare a bulleted list that the manager can quickly look at to see specific items that have improved your area of responsibility. Also include items that have contributed to the success of the overall business. Consider what specific information you'd include on an evaluation for a member of your department who did an excellent job on deployment. Include similar information: figures, numbers, direct examples in your list for your manager.

▸ When you are talking about a raise, your personal financial issues are the least important part of the conversation closely followed by your feelings. It is most important to lay out a case that shows your contributions exceed your compensation. This case should be based on facts so that anyone could look at it and decide that you should be given a raise. Here is an example of both types of conversations. Think about what your decision would be if you were a manager with a very limited budget for raises for all employees.

SCENARIO ONE:

You: "I wanted to talk to you about a pay increase."

Manager: "Ok."

You: "I need a raise because I have lots of bills: car, apartment, loans. I need to make more money, so I wanted to talk to you."

Manager: "I can't do anything right now to help you. I'm sorry."

You: "Well, I'm going to have to get another job at night just to pay my bills if I don't get some more money."

Manager: "Well, do what you have to do. You do have a bright future here, but I can't do anything right now to help you out."

You: "Well, I got a call from a recruiter yesterday, and they said that they had an opportunity that would pay me ten percent more."

Manager: "Well, I'd hate to lose you, but I understand you need to do what's best for you. We only do increases every two years, so we can talk again in six months."

SCENARIO TWO:

You: "I wanted to talk to you about a pay increase."

Manager: "Ok."

You: "I pulled this info for you to look at. It is an executive summary of the steps I have taken that have contributed to a 22 percent increase in productivity within my group. I also included some of the other contributions I have made to the overall growth of the company. The overall business has increased by 12 percent, and I believe we can continue that trend."

Manager: "Wow, this is very impressive."

You: "Thanks. Based on our overall numbers, I estimate these changes have saved us close to three million dollars and increased our revenues by over seven million."

Manager: "Well, you certainly put together some impressive information here."

You: "Given the savings of 3 million and the revenue increase of 7 million, I have positively affected the business by over 10 million dollars. I would like to get my compensation in line with my contribution."

Manager: "Well, we have limited money in the budget for raises; I would like to do something to help you but I'm not sure what my boss will approve."

You: "I understand the limited budget, but I would think you would have a strong case for an increase with the info I have given you. Would it make sense for us to talk to your boss together?"

Manager: "No, I'll handle it. What kind of increase are we talking about?"

In scenario one, the conversation is based on things that don't directly bring value to the business, so the first conversation is about the manager helping the employee. The second scenario is based on the value the employee brought to the business: tangible benefits to the business. If you want to increase your pay, you need highlight your value to the company first so that the conversation is about the business first and you second. Always base your conversations on value to the business because if you are a valuable asset to the business, the manager will want to keep you motivated to continue being valuable. Often managers won't really be aware of your contributions or haven't considered the true value that you bring, so it is up to you to remind them and detail the logic of the increase.

► Subtly selling to set up for a raise or promotion. Subtle selling should occur every day. To do this, you need to time the conversation correctly. You should only bring up quick bits of information to remind people of your value at the appropriate times. This technique is more effective because it is not a long drawn out conversation where you look like a self-promoter. Quick casual reminders can be very effective in detailing your value. Here are a few examples.

Manager: "We exceeded out targets this month!"

You: "By how much?"

Manager: "25%."

You: "I wonder how much the new salesperson we hired to sell new business accounts contributed."

Manager: "It looks like she was seventy-five percent of the increase."

You: "Great, we have been doing weekly meetings and calls to new customers together. If she has increased the business that much so far, I'm excited to see how much we can improve the business next month."

Manager: "Me too!"

You: "I have been spending three hours a week teaching her my process, but I think with that kind of success, I will spend four hours a week with her."

Manager: "That would be great! You are really doing a great job with her. Keep it up."

This kind of conversation is great because it reminds the manager of your contribution and how it directly affects the overall goals of the organization and directly benefits him or her. It is important not to "tell" because again "telling" is less valuable. The conversation where the manager needs to consider everything you are discussing and respond to you with tangible value-based answers makes a big difference. This is the type of information that you can reference on your executive summary during a performance review or pay increase discussion.

▶ Selling others: Whether you are trying to sell as a manager or you are selling an idea to another colleague, you will need to be able to sell others on completing tasks. As previously stated, "telling" someone to do something is very ineffective. You may have had experience with being "told" in the military, but you will quickly learn in the civilian world that people do not respond in the same way. Expectations are very different outside of the service. They may do it, but if they don't believe doing the task is valuable to them, they will just go through the motions and not really complete the task effectively. If you are a manager, selling employees is almost the same process you used before when selling your manager on an idea. However, unlike that situation, you must leave the conversation with the employee completely buying into the implementation of the idea. When you were selling to your manager, you were completing the implementation of hiring someone so the only person who needed to believe in completing the task was you. When you leave the conversation and you need another employee to do something, he or she is the one who needs to complete the task; therefore, he or she must buy in. This is a process that takes time to learn and is often difficult for veterans. We are accustomed to either being told what to do or telling someone else what to do and the task getting done. In order to be effective, take the time to learn the art of selling. Understand that in order to get things done at your new job, you will need to learn to speak to people in a new way.

Here is an example of the process:

Ask a question: "What do we need to do to get those reports out?"

Listen to the answer: "I need to pull the data first and then put it together, but I'm swamped right now."

Repeat the key points: "Ok, so you still need to pull the data and put it together, but you are too busy." Check for a mutual understanding: "Is that right?"

"Yes. That's right."

Ask about the effect of non-resolution: "What will happen if we don't get the reports out?"

"We will probably all be looking for new jobs since the report is for the CEO."

Repeat the effect: "Ok, so we will all be looking for new jobs?"

"Probably! I'm so stressed out!"

Ask about the options: "What options do we have?"

"None! I am the only one who can pull the data, and I am stuck here at the reception desk since Dave is out. The phone won't stop ringing, and I have to log every call in the system!"

Repeat the key options: "So, you are the only one who can pull the data, and you have to answer phones for Dave and log calls?" Ask about your idea: "What if I answer calls and log them in the system for you while you focus on getting the report done?"

Listen: "Well that might work, but no one else knows how to log calls, and it would take me a month to teach you."

Ask clarifying questions: "Do the calls need to be logged as they come in, or could they be logged at the end of the day or tomorrow?"

"It is just for sales leads, so they can be logged whenever."

"Are there any compliance or other legal issues with logging the calls the next day, rather than right away?"

"No, there are no compliance or legal issues as this is simply something, I track to help provide information to the sales reps."

State your solution idea: "Ok, how about I answer the calls and write down the info in Excel, and then you can log them tomorrow after the deadline for the report to the CEO. That way we can all keep our jobs."

Ask for the opportunity to work toward reaching an agreement: "Ok, can we make this work, so we can get the report done?"

"Sure, but let me know if you get stuck, ok?"

"No problem. Can you definitely get that report done?"

"I'll do it; I guess it is the most important thing we can do today."

"Well besides losing our job, our CEO needs the info to get funding from the bank so we can expand our bank lines. That will make the difference between the business's success and failure next year."

"Wow, I didn't realize that!"

"Yes, so your report matters a lot."

"I'm on it right now."

This scenario is typical in any field; people often don't prioritize and just do what is in front of them. You will often have to convince someone to do something, but simply telling him or her will not be effective. You need to first connect and reach a mutual understanding of the issues. Once you both understand the issue, you can work toward a resolution. If you don't ask questions, you will not have a clear view of the whole situation, and without posing questions, the person you are talking to may not have thought about the situation and the implications of non-resolution.

▶ Pointing out others' faults subtly: To point out faults subtly requires tact and discretion. It is important to not publicly point out shortcomings. If you have to do so, the best way of handling the conversation is to offer a theoretical reason for the other person not doing something. This way you are not saying, "He is a slacker!" or "She doesn't care whether she is late to work!" or "He doesn't mind being average!"

A way to point out shortcomings without passing judgment could look like this:

"With the workload everyone has this week, he probably had more pressing things to do."

or "The construction on the interstate has made traffic un-bearable. I bet she will be here soon,"

or "He always seems so content."

▶ By pointing out the shortcomings in a positive way, you don't look like you are trying to point them out. The other person to whom you are talking can then choose to accept the theoretical reason or read between the lines. Either way, you should not do this often and only when necessary.

▶ Defending against others pointing out your faults: If some-one attacks you in a public meeting or any type of public setting and looks to you for a response, it can be very uncomfortable for everyone in the room. The best way to handle the situation is to immediately end the public discussion and take it "offline." If you just take it offline though, people will assume it is true. A quick response first may be appropriate to maintain continuity of the conversation before the comment. One way to do this is as follows:

Attacker: "Well, your team took forever to get the report to the CEO. We almost lost our bank line!"

You: "I'm afraid you don't have all of the information; I think this discussion is outside the context of this conversa-tion, so let's discuss it privately."

The attacker should choose to accept your response particularly if the comment is outside the context of the conversation, but if he or she doesn't, you may need to respond. If you need to discuss the issue in front of others, succinctly address the issue. Be sure to be unemotional and simply list the facts.

Attacker: "Well, I think this is the appropriate venue and audience for discussion."

You: Smile and reply, "Sure. We were two people short in the office that day and needed to shuffle responsibilities to get it done. We did that and got the report out on time. It required some overtime, and I had to answer phones in addition to my other responsibilities, but the team pulled together well, and we got the bank line."

This should thwart the attacker but if it doesn't, you may need to simply cut the conversation off.

Attacker: "Well, you could have started sooner!"

You: "Well, I'm sure we can all make improvements. Let's not waste everyone's time on this issue. I'll be available after the meeting if you have additional suggestions."

That response needs to be firm. If done correctly, the attacker will look like he is wasting everyone's time by trying to call you out on something that is irrelevant.

Tips:

▶ Learn to sell yourself through concrete examples of your contributions.

▶ Understand that civilians do not respond in the same way as service members to being commanded to do something. Learn the art of selling and communicating to increase productivity from your team.

CHAPTER SIXTEEN
CONCLUSION

I WANTED TO KEEP this book short and to the point. Remember to always listen, connect, and develop a mutual understanding with those around you regardless of what you are doing.

▸ From interviewing to management, connecting to develop a mutual understanding is the most important skill one can develop.

▸ From interviewing to selling ideas, always take some time to prepare and develop a solid plan.

▸ Don't forget to ask questions, and never simply tell people what to do when you are trying to convince them of your opinion.

▸ Never stop learning, continue to reflect every day on your personal and professional goals, and always keep the value of your personal brand in mind.

ABOUT THE AUTHORS

KEVIN LACZ was born and raised in central Connecticut before enrolling in James Madison University in 2000. When the terrorist attacks on September 11, 2001 claimed the life of a good friend's father, he decided to leave school in favor of military service with the aim to become a Navy SEAL. He graduated BUD/S with Class 246 and also attended 18D Special Operations Combat Medic School at Fort Bragg before checking into SEAL Team THREE in Coronado, California. Kevin Completed two combat deployments to Iraq (2006 and 2008) with SEAL Team THREE (Charlie and Delta platoons) as a platoon sniper, breacher, and combat medic. His platoon's 2006 deployment to Ramadi, then the most dangerous city in Iraq, has been discussed in several books, including Chris Kyle's *American Sniper* and Dick Couch's *The Sheriff of Ramadi*. Kevin's presence in *Sniper* led to his involvement in the production of and eventual casting in the Oscar nominated Clint Eastwood directed Chris Kyle biopic by the same name (starring Bradley Cooper).

Upon completing his enlistment, Kevin was honorably discharged from the Navy. He was awarded a number of commendations for his service, including a Bronze Star with a combat 'V'. He completed a degree in Political Science in 2011 from UCONN and a Masters of Health Sciences from Wake Forest University. Currently, Kevin works as a Physician Assistant in Pensacola. He enjoys using his past experiences to facilitate his work in medicine and charity. His military service influences him greatly as he seeks to actively support service members and veterans in his community. Kevin is happy to have found a home in Florida with his wife, Lindsey, and two young children.

BILL HOBBS is a bestselling author and the creator of *The WORK Book Series*. Drawing from his extensive business knowledge as an employer and employee in the Fortune 500 and Start-up worlds, Bill wrote *The WORK Book* which encourages students to discover and build their personal brands. *The WORK Book* has become required reading at top universities around the country. Bill is also the co-author of the *Hacking the Internship Process*, and the co-author of *The Veteran's WORK Book*.

As a business leader, Bill has built top performing sales teams in the Fortune 500 world, led large scale business transformations, market expansions, and delivered consistent growth for software companies in New York and Silicon Valley. Bill has served on the Board of Advisors for several leading software companies and has been named to the "Top 100 Global Sales Leaders List" as well as the "Top 100 Customer Success Strategists List."

LINDSEY LACZ is the co-author of Amazon and New York Times Bestselling Iraq War memoir *The Last Punisher*. She earned a BA from the University of North Carolina at Chapel Hill in 2004 and a Master of Arts in Education from the College of William & Mary in 2005. Although she began her career as a high school social studies teacher, her lifelong interest in military history eventually redirected her to writing for the contemporary military and veteran audience. In addition to writing, Lindsey works actively with current and former service members through the non-profit she co-founded, Hunting for Healing.

Lindsey lives in Florida with her husband, Kevin, and two young children.

ACKNOWLEDGEMENTS

T HE WORK BOOK SERIES would like to thank Howard Schragin for his legal consultation on *The Veterans' Work Book*.

HOWARD SCHRAGIN is a founding partner of Sapir Schragin LLP, a boutique employment law firm, and is an experienced labor and employment attorney who handles a wide range of labor and employment matters on behalf of employees and employers.

Mr. Schragin is a member of the New York State Bar Association, Labor and Employment Law Section, New York City Bar Association, and Westchester County Bar Association. He has written and spoken for various organizations on a range of employment law topics, including the Family and Medical Leave Act, Americans with Disabilities Act, separation agreements and restrictive covenants, employment hiring practices, genetic discrimination, pre-employment drug, medical, and psychological testing, electronic and digital media in the workplace, and human resources best practices. Mr. Schragin is a contributor to "New York Employment Law" and wrote the chapter on New York wage and hour law. He was also a frequent contributor to the New York Employment Newsletter.

Mr. Schragin is a graduate of the University of Wisconsin-Madison and Fordham University School of Law, where he was a Notes & Articles Editor for the Fordham International Law Journal.

APPENDIX 1: RÉSUMÉ

JOHN DOE
1234 Sample St Example FL 32563
H: 000-000-0000 example@example.com

Summary
10-year member of the USMC with leadership experience ranging from small groups to more than 200 personnel. Seeking opportunities in the private sector in management to share the organization's mission.

Skills

- Excellent communication
- Operations management
- Results-oriented
- Training and development

- Quick learner
- Time management skills
- Multi-Task Management

Experience

Staff Sergeant 02/2014 to Current US Marine Corps Lansing, MI

- Patrolled areas and allowed restricted area access for authorized personnel.
- Maintained rifles, machine guns, mortars, and hand grenades.
- Commanded more than 85 arms combat patrols on foot and in vehicles.
- Served as the principal platoon officer for all matters concerning training and the use of all weapons systems.
- Received and implemented combat orders and directed deployment of personnel in offensive, defensive, and retrograde operations.
- Planned and assembled training and logistics packets for deployments and redeployments.

Sergeant 01/2013 to 02/2014 US Marine Corps Quantico, VA

- Advised, trained, and developed leadership and military tactics for foreign personnel.
- Responsible for training 150-200 person unit.
- Responsible for $12million of equipment

Platoon Sergeant 11/2011 to 12/2012 US Marine Corps Camp Pendleton, CA

- Commanded operations post, including personnel, weapons, and equipment.
- Coordinated operations with armor, artillery, and air support units.

**Team Leader 09/2009 to 08/2007 US Marine Corps Camp
Pendleton, CA**

Education and Training

**Associate of Arts: Business 2006 Pensacola State College
Pensacola, FL, United States**

- Dean's List Honoree Fall 2005, Spring 2006
- 3.8 GPA

Activities and Honors

- 2 Bronze Star Medals with 'V'
- 2 Navy and Marine Corps Commendation Medals
- 5 Navy and Marine Corps Achievement Medals